Making a Stand

Tony Bradman ■ Jonatronix

OXFORD
UNIVERSITY PRESS

Previously ...

Dani Day, a scientist working at NASTI, finds out about Dr X's evil plans. She takes a micro-watch, shrinks and goes into hiding.

Dani realizes that Max, Cat, Ant and Tiger have the other micro-watches. She goes to warn them that they might be in danger.

The children fend off an X-bot attack.

Dr X is defeated … or is he?

Chapter 1 – The elite X-bots

It was the sound that alerted Dani Day. *CLICK, CLACK, CLICK* it went, followed by a strange humming noise. Micro-sized Dani peeked out of her hiding place.

Deep underground, in the secret headquarters of NASTI (Nano Science and Technology Inc) an elite squad of X3-bots was gathering. Dr X watched them. He smiled a very satisfied smile. His henchmen, Plug and Socket, stood beside him, grinning. For once, the boss was in a good mood.

Finally the last X-bot took its place … and the whole squad stood still. The clicking and clacking and humming stopped.

Dr X reached out and pressed a button on the control panel in front of him. Pictures of Max, Cat, Ant and Tiger instantly appeared on the giant screen. The X-bots turned to look, their robot heads all moving as one.

"X-bots!" yelled Dr X. "You know what you have to do." He pointed up at the screen and hopped up and down with excitement. "Now go and do it!"

For a brief moment nothing happened. Dani hoped something had gone wrong with the X-bots. Maybe the computer chips inside them had crashed.

But then they suddenly hummed and fizzed into robot life. They marched out of the room, *CLICK*, *CLACK*, *CLICK*, a river of shiny black chrome.

Dani crawled out of her hiding place and followed the X-bots. She kept to the shadows so she wouldn't be seen. She had to know what Dr X was planning. Then she must find a way to warn Max, Cat, Ant and Tiger.

Eventually the X-bots arrived at a place Dani recognized. It was the room where Dr X had kept his super-cool X-pod – the one Dani had borrowed to visit the children. But the X-pod had gone. Up on the plinth, where the X-pod had been, was a much larger flying machine. It had room for a whole squad of X-bots. Dani shuddered.

She watched in horror as the X-bots marched up the ramp and into the X-craft …

Dani thought about charging up the ramp and into the X-craft. But it was guarded by two very mean-looking X-bots and she couldn't tackle them on her own. Dr X had obviously increased his security.

Dani watched helplessly as the doors in the ceiling of the room slid open. The X-bot guards sealed the doors and the X-craft blasted off.

Dani had a bad feeling that the X-craft was heading for the children's den. What could she do?

High up on a bench across the room, Dani could just see a computer terminal. The X-bots had gone and the room was empty. There was only one thing for it. She turned the dial on her watch, pushed the X and grew back to her normal size.

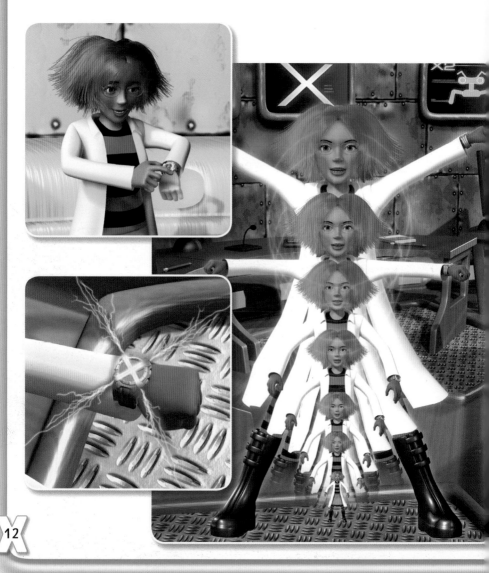

The only way to be sure where the X-craft was going was to hack into the main NASTI computer. She hurried across to the terminal and began tapping away at the keyboard.

"Come on," she said to herself urgently.

But it wasn't easy. Dr X had altered all the codes and she couldn't find a way in. He had obviously increased his computer security, too.

Now Dani had a dilemma. If she wasn't quick, she could get caught. Then Dr X would discover she had been hiding out at NASTI. He had been very suspicious when his X-pod had mysteriously disappeared … and then reappeared. But she had to do something to warn the children.

ACCESS DENIED

She had to try something else. Maybe she could get a message to Max using her watch. She stepped away from the computer and began to fiddle with the dial. Finally the watch face glowed with a bright purple light. She leaned forward and spoke into the light …

"Max! Max! Can you hear me? It's me, Dani. You're in danger …"

The light fizzled out before she could say any more. She just hoped the message had got through.

Then Dani turned the dial on her watch, pushed the X and shrank back down to micro-size. She hurried back to her hiding place in an air vent in the NASTI control room. All she could do now was to keep watching Dr X.

She had no idea that she was being watched by the smallest spy-bot in the world – a nano-bot.

Chapter 2 – Two grumpy men

Plug and Socket's day had started well. The boss had been in a good mood. They had stood beside him as he watched the X-craft take off. He had laughed and laughed and laughed. But then, for no reason at all, Dr X had lost his temper. He had yelled at Plug and Socket about their *incompetence*, whatever that was. Then he had given them a long list of boring jobs to do.

"How come we have to clean the drains again?" grumbled Plug. He pulled on his red and white apron and grabbed the cleaning things.

"I don't know," said Socket, with a shrug. "Maybe the boss thinks there's something important down there."

"As if …" muttered Plug. "I think he just likes to make us suffer."

"Yeah," Socket said gloomily. "Come on."

The pair of them headed off to the NASTI drains …

They worked silently for a while, mopping up the vile, smelly muck that had collected in the drains.

At last Plug gave a big sigh and put down his broom.

"You know, this isn't what I signed up for when I joined NASTI," he muttered. "I thought it was going to be all adventure and excitement."

"Me too," said Socket. He leant on his mop. "'*We'll take over the world*', the boss said."

"Ah, but he was different then," said Plug. "Do you remember when we were his only friends at school?"

"Yes. Everybody else was horrible to him ... calling him *Shorty* and stuff ... and now he's being horrible to us!" cried Socket. "He told us we were going to rule the world!"

"Instead of which we're just ... cleaners," said Plug, sounding very grumpy indeed. "Well, I'm fed up with it!"

"So am I!" said Socket. "And I think we ought to do something."

"But what?" asked Plug.

"I know!" exclaimed Socket. "We could take over and run NASTI ourselves. We don't need Dr X!"

"I like your thinking!" said Plug, sounding much more cheerful. "We just tell the boss that we're not working for him any more."

"Then we take control ourselves … HA! HA!"

Plug and Socket danced wildly around, splashing slime all over the walls of the drain. They were happy for the first time in ages.

"Hang on a second," said Plug. He stopped dancing. "We can't just stroll up to Dr X and tell him he's sacked."

"You're right. He's more likely to sack us!"

"And he's got his new *elite squad* … they're the meanest X-bots yet."

"I hadn't thought of that," groaned Socket.

The two of them stared gloomily at the muck and slime. The drains were cold and dark and silent.

Then, suddenly, Plug looked at Socket. Socket looked at Plug.

"Are you thinking what I'm thinking?" whispered Plug.

"I might be," said Socket, smiling.

"Didn't we just see the elite squad leave on the X-craft?" said Plug.

"Yes, we did," said Socket.

"So, what are we hanging about down here doing the cleaning for?"

"Let's go!" cried Socket.

Flinging their brooms, mops and aprons down, Plug and Socket ran out of the drain. They had no idea they were being watched by the smallest spy-bot in the world …

Chapter 3 – A garbled message

Max, Cat, Ant and Tiger turned the dials on their watches. They pushed the X and …

Things were quiet at the old tree stump in the park. It was a hot and sultry day. The air was thick, as if a storm was coming.

The children were just hanging out in their micro-den. Max and Cat were changing the feather blades on the micro-copter. Tiger was writing a list of all the things he still wanted to do with his amazing micro-watch. After their meeting with Dani Day, Tiger was worried that his watch would be taken away.

Then Ant remembered he had some good news.

"My mum and dad said that tonight is OK," he told the others. "They've agreed to let us sleep in a tent in the garden!"

Ant had found out that a comet would be visible in the sky that night. He had asked his parents if his friends could stay over so they could all watch it together.

"That's great!" said Max. "At least we've got something fun to look forward to."

"What's that supposed to mean?" snapped Cat. "Do we always have to be doing something smelly or dirty or dangerous? It's fun just being here."

"Well, I am a bit bored," muttered Tiger. "And I've got a list of smelly and dirty things I want to do while I'm micro-size."

"And what if that spider gets you this time?" said Cat.

Tiger turned red. He was terrified of spiders.

adventure in mud
sail on puddle
explore rabbit hole

Suddenly there was a loud *BLEEP!* Everybody jumped. Max's watch glowed with a bright blue light. Then a face appeared in the light. It was Dani Day!

"Max! Max! Can you hear me? It's me, Dani. You're in danger …"

No sooner than it had started, the message fizzled and died. The light on Max's watch went out.

"What does it mean?" said Tiger.

"More trouble, I think," said Ant.

"Make it play again, Max!" cried Cat.

Max fiddled with his watch and eventually Dani's face glowed out of the screen again. But this time Dani's voice sounded strange and mechanical. All it said was: *"Max! 888100 … Dani …86594 … danger."*

"What's going on?" asked Cat, looking worried.

"I think someone must have intercepted the message. It's been scrambled," said Ant.

All four children shuddered. They knew that Dani was inside NASTI keeping watch on Dr X. She had taken a big risk trying to send them a message.

"Max," said Cat, as calmly as she could. "What do we do?"

For the first time since they had found the watches, the children were truly scared.

Max wanted to put them on full alert for an X-bot attack. Tiger said his watch wasn't flashing, so there couldn't be any X-bots around. He was all for going back down the drains and launching an attack on NASTI. Cat wanted to try and get a message back to Dani. Ant didn't think it would get through. And if Dr X intercepted it, it might put Dani in danger.

Soon, instead of working together, the four friends were arguing loudly about what to do.

"Right!" shouted Max, finally. "We can't just hang out here waiting for the X-bots to find us. Let's go to Ant's house. We'll be safe normal size … and Dani might send us another message."

Cat, Ant and Tiger agreed. The four friends crept out of their micro-den, turned the dials on their watches and were soon normal size. They set off for Ant's house.

Little did they know they were being watched. The nano-bot was far too small to be detected, even by Tiger's watch …

Chapter 4 – Scary X-bots!

Plug and Socket's day was getting worse by the second. They certainly weren't running along any more. Instead they were stumbling and splashing in the dark, up to their knees in smelly water.

"I thought you said you knew which way to go!" moaned Plug.

"I thought I did!" groaned Socket.

"But if you don't that means we could be trapped in these drains forever!" cried Plug.

"Wait a second," said Socket. "There's a light at the end of this tunnel."

"You're right," said Plug. "It could be the way out. Let's head in that direction."

"Er … I don't think we need to," said Socket, peering into the darkness. "The light seems to be heading towards us."

All of a sudden, a whole army of X-bots appeared. A hundred eyes glowed red.

"X-bots!" cried Socket. "What are they doing down here? I thought most of them had gone off in the X-craft."

"I hope they're not after our cleaning jobs," said Plug. "Nasty little things ..."

"You certainly wouldn't want to meet one down a dark tunnel," said Socket. He looked around him at the dark tunnel. Then he looked at Plug.

"Run for it!" they both yelled together.

The X-bots poured down the drain towards Plug and Socket. The tunnel was full of the sound of metal jaws clicking and clacking.

Before long, they came to the entrance. When they finally scrambled out of the slime Dr X was waiting for them ...

Meanwhile ...

Dani Day crouched down in her hiding place, wondering whether her message had got through. Maybe she should try sending another one. Just then she heard an ominous sound outside. It was the humming and clicking and clacking of an X-bot.

She peered out through the air vent and gulped. The mean-looking X-bots that had been guarding the X-craft were right outside! There was no time to think – she had only one choice to make, and that was to run.

The metal grill covering the air vent fell aside with a clang. The clicking and clacking of X-bot feet echoed down the tunnel. Dani did her best to escape. She ducked and dived, she dodged and jumped but it was no use. The X-bots surrounded her. At micro-size she was helpless. They grabbed her in their metal jaws and carried her back to the control room. Dr X was waiting for her …

"So, we meet again, Miss Day," said Dr X, grinning. He loomed over Dani like a giant. "You'd better return to your normal size so we can talk properly."

There was nothing Dani could do. She turned the dial on her watch, pushed the X and grew back to normal.

Then she noticed Plug and Socket in the corner of the room. They were covered in slime and shivering uncontrollably.

"Having trouble with your staff?" she mocked. "Well, that's no surprise. You never were much good as a boss."

"I don't think you're in a position to make jokes, Miss Day," growled Dr X. His grin vanished and he scowled. "Now, hand over that watch …"

Chapter 5 – One last trick

"What happens if I don't?" said Dani. She clutched at the purple watch on her wrist and stared down at Dr X defiantly. She tried hard to sound a lot braver than she felt. "You can't make me."

"Oh, I'm sure I can," said Dr X. He clicked his fingers and the scary X-bots moved forward.

"I suppose you could run, or shrink, or do any of a hundred things. But in the time it takes you to make up your mind, I'll have made my move. You're as bad as those two idiots over there."

"What's he talking about?" said Plug, confused. Dr X turned to face his former henchmen.

"I'm talking about why I will rule the world, while you'll still be thinking about what to have for lunch!" he cried. "I make decisions! And the best decision I ever made was to keep an eye on all of you …"

Dr X held out his hand and showed them the nano-bot. "I've known for ages that you were still here, Miss Day. And that Plug and Socket were restless and grumpy. They even thought they could take over NASTI! But while you were wrestling with your dilemmas, I was being utterly decisive!"

"What do you mean?" said Dani.

"You know what I mean, Miss Day," Dr X smirked. "You were there when the X-craft took off. My X-bot army is on its way to find those children. I'm going to get my watches back. Then the world had better look out!"

"You won't get away with this, Dr X!" said Dani. "You're not nearly as clever as you think. Those kids are far too sharp for you!"

"Is that so?" said Dr X. "Well, let me show you something …"

He pushed a button on the control panel and the giant screen filled with pictures of Max, Cat, Ant and Tiger. The children were setting up a tent in a garden.

"Look! Your friends are all together in the open. They're waiting for a message from you, I think. How sweet! But what you forgot to tell them is that my elite squad of X-bots is on its way. They won't let me down. This time, I *will* get my watches back. I'll start by taking that one from you now."

Dani slowly undid the purple watch and held it out towards Dr X. His eyes glittered as he reached for it. But Dani had one last trick up her sleeve.

"OK ... here it is!" she cried, and threw the watch into the air.

A look of panic passed across Dr X's face. Time seemed to stand still. He needed to get the watch and he needed to stop Dani.

"CATCH IT!" he shouted to his X-bots. "STOP HER YOU FOOLS!" he screamed at Plug and Socket.

But they were too late. Dani sprinted across the room, dodging the scuttling X-bots. She flung herself through the door and ran as fast as she could. She had to help the children.

She only hoped that Max, Cat, Ant and Tiger were ready for what was coming.

To be continued . . .

Next time ...

Will Dr X's plan succeed?

Will Max, Cat, Ant and Tiger see the comet?

Will they get captured by the X-craft?

Or will the micro-friends defeat the X-bots?

Find out more ...

Read more about dilemmas and decisions in ...

The Missing Statue

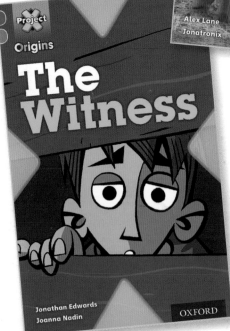

and *The Witness*